Dedicated to

Mikhail S. Gorbachev · Andrei D. Sakharov

with great love

BHAGWAN
SHREE
RAJNEESH

ON
BASIC HUMAN RIGHTS

Two Discourses
given on December 25 and 28, 1986
in Bombay, India

First Edition: January 1987 – 5,000 copies
Published by: Rajneesh Foundation Europe

Printed in Germany

ISBN 3-907757-03-3

"Beloved Bhagwan,

It feels strange when the establishment, worldwide, which is ever busy with all its efforts and resources to make sure in every possible way that man cannot remain man, asks us to celebrate "Human Rights Day." Goodness, what is all this that's going on?

Beloved Master, would You care to explain?"

One of the most fundamental things to be always remembered is that we are living in a hypocrite society.

Once, a great philosopher was asked: "What do you think of civilization?"

The philosopher said, "It is a good idea, but somebody has to change the idea into a reality. Civilization has not happened yet. It is a dream of the future."

But the people who are in power – politically, religiously, socially – are in power because civilization has not happened. A civilized world, a mature man, needs no nations – all those boundaries are false – needs no religions, because all those theologies are simple fictions.

The people who have been for thousands of years in power – the priests, the politicians, the super-rich – have all the powers to prevent human evolution. But the best way to prevent it is to convince man, "You are already civilized," to convince man, "You are already a human being. You need not go through a transformation, it is unnecessary."

And man's weakness is that knowing perfectly well there exists no such thing as civilization, there exists no such thing as human sensitivity, still he starts believing in all the lies that the politicans have been speaking, the priests have been preaching, the educationists have been teaching, because it seems simpler to just believe – you don't have to do anything for it.

To recognize the fact that you are not yet a man creates fear. The very ground underneath your feet disappears.

Truth makes you utterly naked – naked of all lies, naked of all hypocrisies. That's why nobody wants truth; everybody believes that he has *got* it.

Do you see the psychological strategy? If you don't want to give something to someone, convince him, hypnotize, repeat again and again, "You have got it." And when thousands of people around you – your parents, your teachers, your priests, your leaders – are all believing it, it seems almost impossible for new arrivals in the world, small children, not to be convinced of this thousands-of-years-old idea. Millions of people have lived and died believing that civilization has happened.

So the first thing I want you to understand is that we are still barbarous. Only barbarians can do things that we have been doing for thousands of years – not human beings. In three thousand years, five thousand wars ... and you call man civilized?

In the twentieth century – exactly in the middle of the twentieth century – you can produce Adolf Hitler, you can produce Josef Stalin, you can produce Benito Mussolini, you can produce Mao Tse-tung, and still you believe man is civilized?

Adolf Hitler alone killed six million human beings, and killed with great sophistication. Science and technology have been used. One million Jews have been simply burned in gas chambers – within seconds thousands of people are nothing but smoke going out of the chimneys. He killed so many people that it was impossible to give each person the conventional grave.

Man has never been so poor – even beggars have graves, but he had killed so many people that to make graves for all of them ... the whole of Germany would have became a graveyard. So he had deep ditches prepared, and people were simply thrown into the ditches and covered with mud.

Before throwing their bodies in the ditches he destroyed even those dead peoples' dignity. Their clothes were taken away; their heads, their beards, their moustaches were shaved so you could not recognize the face of the person. Their heads were cut off; so you would find somewhere the head and somewhere the hand and somewhere the leg and somewhere the remaining parts of the body. And thousands of people – it was impossible to figure out who you were looking for.

Why did he do that? So that nobody could be recognized. Even if somebody was dead, he could not be recognized; he did not even have his whole body. And you say that man is civilized?

And this is not the end of the story. Seeing the second world war, one would have thought that just a little intelligence is needed and the second world war should be the last world war – seeing what man himself has been doing to man. But no, we are preparing for the third world war – and the last.

Albert Einstein was asked, "Can you say something about what is going to happen in the third world war?"

And Einstein said, "Excuse me, I cannot say anything about the third world war, but I can say something about the fourth."

The questioner could not believe it. He said, "You cannot say anything about the third – and it is so complicated – yet you are ready to say something about the fourth, which will be even more complicated!"

Albert Einstein said, "You don't understand. I can say something definitively, categorically, about the fourth. And that is that the fourth is never going to happen, because the third will destroy all life – not only human beings, roses too. All that is living will disappear from the earth."

And you say that humanity has become civilized? No, you have been deceived and this Universal Declaration of Human Rights by the United Nations is nothing but the same hypocrisy.

George Gurdjieff used to tell a small story – but it is about humanity. The story is that there was a magician. He lived deep in the mountains and the forests, and he had thousands of sheep. But the problem was that the sheep were afraid of the magician because every day the sheep were seeing that one of them was being killed for his breakfast, another was being killed for his lunch. So they used to run away from the magician's place, and it was a difficult job to find them in the vast forest. Being a magician, he used magic. He hypnotized all the sheep and told different sheep ... to some, "You are a man, you need not be afraid. It is only the sheep who are going to be killed and eaten, not *you.* You are a man just like I am."

Some other sheep were told, "You are a lion – only sheep are afraid. They escape, they are cowards. You are a lion; you would prefer to die than to run away. You don't belong to these sheep, so when they are killed it is not your problem. They are *meant* to be killed, but you are the most loved of my friends in this forest."

In this way he told all the sheep different stories, and from the second day, the sheep stopped running away from the house. They still saw other sheep being killed, butchered, but it was not their concern. Somebody was a lion, somebody was a tiger, somebody was a man, somebody was.... Nobody was a sheep except the one who was being killed.

This way, without keeping servants, he managed thousands of sheep. They would go into the forest for their food, for their water, and they would come back home, believing always one thing: "It is some sheep who is going to be killed, not *you*. You don't belong to this mob. You are a lion – respected, honored, a friend of the great magician." The problems of the magician were solved.

I am telling you this story because it is literally true about you. You are being told things, and you accept them without even looking all around to see whether those things coincide with the reality or not.

The first thing... My first objection to the U.N.'s Declaration of Human Rights is that rights exist only when there are duties. Duties are roots, rights are the flowers; you cannot have rights without duties. And to celebrate a day in the year for human rights ... but they don't celebrate a day for human duties, which come first.

Why are they not talking about human duties? Because they don't want to give you your human rights. Without duties, rights can only be talked about but you won't have them in your hands. And about duties, these politicians who have made this declaration have no notion at all. I will give you a few examples.

They say that every human being is equal. And of course it satisfies the ego of every human being – nobody objects. It is one of the most dangerous lies to tell human beings.

I say to you, equality is a myth.

There are not even two human beings who are equal – in *any* way, in any dimension. I don't mean that they are unequal, I mean that they are unique, incomparable, so the question of equality or inequality does not arise. Are you equal to these pillars in the hall? The pillars may be beautiful, but you are not equal to them. But does that mean you are inferior to the pillars? It simply means you are not a pillar – pillars are pillars, you are you.

Every human being is a category unto himself.

And unless we recognize the uniqueness of each individual, there are not going to be any human rights and there is not going to be a civilized world – human, loving, rejoicing.

In the declaration they emphasized the fact again and again that you should love all human beings; you are all brothers. But have you ever seen brothers being in love? Have you ever seen brothers being friends? The way brothers fight, nobody fights. And just saying, "You are brothers," does not make it a reality. These people who declared these human rights – what authority have they got? Who are they? Politicans … and they are the cause of all the wars, they are the cause of all kinds of violence happening all over the world.

These are the people who have kept almost half of humanity – womankind – in a state of slavery. But looking at the declaration I had really a great time … because it does not talk about sisters, only brothers.

Sisters don't count – yet they are half of humanity.

They are not even mentioned.

These politicians are articulate, clever, cunning … mostly coming from the legal profession. They are saying there should be no discrimination between man and woman, between black and white. Between races, religions, political ideologies, there should be no discrimination. And who is making the discrimination? These are the same people who are making the declaration.

They have enslaved the woman for centuries, and they are not yet willing to give her freedom – which, according to their declaration, is a basic human right.

The blacks are being treated as animals. Just at the end of the last century the blacks were still being sold, auctioned in marketplaces like a commodity. And even today, they are not respected as the white people are respected.

And these are the white people – all these politicians are white. These white people have been driving the whole of humanity, for three hundred years, into slavery. They all had their empires. England had the biggest empire; it was said that the sun never set in the British Empire. Somewhere or other in the British Empire the sun was shining and it was day – all around the earth. But other white people were not far behind: the French, the Portugese, the Spanish – they all had vast empires, exploiting the whole earth. They have been the parasites – and it is hilarious that all these parasites are now declaring human rights.

This is a deception. It is not meant; what they are saying they don't mean. It is just to give you an idea that you are equal to everybody, you are a brother to everybody, that you have all the human rights.

But I know – all these human rights are just hypocrisies.

I know by my own experience.

There is one human right enumerated in this declaration: Nobody can be arrested without a warrant. I was arrested exactly like that in America – without a warrant, without any arrest warrant or search warrant. Not even verbally did they inform me what crime I had committed. And when I asked them, "What crime have I committed? I must know at least," the answer was loaded guns – twelve loaded guns surrounding my jet airplane.

When guns are answers, then you can be certain civilization is far away.

They did not have any arrest warrant. The simple thing for the court would have been... but they not only arrested me, they were clever; they deliberately arrested me at such a time that I would have to be in jail for at least two days. On Monday the court would open – only then could I be bailed out. They themselves were certain that I would be bailed out because there was no reason to hold me; they didn't have any proof, any evidence against me. They had chosen a certain situation in which for two days the court was closed – so at least they would have the satisfaction of torturing me for two days. On the third day ... I was not amazed when the court refused to give me bail.

The magistrate, a woman, did not even allow my attorneys to question the fact that I had been arrested without any arrest warrant. In a democratic country which claims to be the greatest democratic country in the world, the court would not allow them even to discuss it, because to discuss it would be an exposure. There was no question of giving me bail. In the first place I had been arrested without any warrant, and even after three days they didn't have the warrant – the question of bail does not arise. The bail was not given.

In the second court, in a higher federal court, again the question: What about my arrest? – which is the basic question – was not discussed. Everything else is secondary. First you arrest somebody without even telling him why he is being arrested....

And in these human rights, these same politicians sitting in America say that nobody can be arrested without an arrest warrant; this is a fundamental human right. If I was not arrested, I might not have known.

They say nobody should interfere in anybody's philosophy, religion, political ideology – that is every individual's birthright.

But my commune in America has been destroyed for the simple reason that Christianity – my being not a white man, my commune being universal.... There were black people, there were people from all over the world. It was the only place where there was no discrimination of any kind. They destroyed a commune which was fulfilling human rights in every detail.

On the surface man has become civilized, but deep in the darker parts of his unconsciousness he is still barbarous.

In the introduction to this declaration it says: We are determined to eliminate all forms of intolerance and of discrimination based on religion or belief. And this is not true in any country. Religions are fighting continuously, and if the government consists of fanatic, religious people, the minority is crushed and destroyed in every possible way. The desire is good, but the people who are desiring it are all wrong.

In the convention at which the U.N. declared these fundamental rights, the Soviet Union was absent; eight other communist countries were absent. America was present. Unanimously the declaration was adopted – all in favor and nobody against. I am mentioning it because it was basically an American initiative to make this declaration. And America is the first to be going against *every* human right.

Just now, America has given two hundred million dollars to the terrorists in Nicaragua, a small country which has become communist, just like Cuba. To destroy the country, America has flooded it with terrorists. Now millions of dollars are being poured in continuously, to support the terrorists with weapons and with everything. And in this declaration it says that every country is sovereign and no other country should interfere in any other country's life, religion. That is *their* business – how they want to live, what they want to believe or not to believe. It is nobody else's business at all. If in some small country people have accepted communism as their lifestyle and their social structure, who is America? – and what right have they?

Nicaragua appealed to the World Court. And the World Court is full of American judges; still the court said to America, "Your act is against the human rights declaration, it is criminal." Ronald Reagan simply cancelled it. He said, "We don't care about the World Court or their decisions." Now these are the people who have made the declaration. They have created the World Court to decide in situations where some conflict arises, and these same people are not ready to listen.

Do you see the politics behind it? The World Court, the declaration – all are facades to hide things. If some small country was doing it, then the World Court would be right, and America would have taken action in support of the court to destroy that country because it was doing a criminal act. Now, because America itself is doing the criminal act, it simply can say, "We don't care about the World Court."

And what can the World Court do? It has no armies, it has no power. It has all the power that has been given to the politicans, but if those politicans themselves go against the laws they have made, what can the court do?

And the U.N. is silent. Its court has been insulted. If the people in the U.N. have any dignity they will dissolve the U.N. and dissolve the World Court – because what is the point? Today America is doing it tomorrow other countries will be doing it. And the Soviet Union is far better, and is right, because it never participated in this declaration. It is not part of this declaration; no communist government participated in it. So at least they have shown from the very beginning that these things are all bogus: "Who are you trying to cheat?"

All the rights are in a way not very rational. For example, in this long declaration, the right to leave the body when one has lived enough and is now weak, sick, old, a burden and of no use... One is suffering unnecessarily and waiting for death. Why wait? Why put this man unnecessarily through torture?

The society is responsible for thousands of people who are in torture – in hospitals or in nursing homes. They don't have any possibility of coming back to life healthy, creative, of any use. But they can go on vegetating; and medicine is developed enough – you can keep them in the hospitals for years. Artificial breathing ... perhaps the man is already dead, but because of the artificial breathing you are deceived.

In this long list, one of the most important human rights is not included and that right is the right to leave the world, to give the ticket back, to say, "I want to go back home. Who are you to prevent me or anybody?"

But that right, which is very significant today because in the advanced countries, the average life span has gone to such lengths that more and more people will be in a situation where their sons and daughters are already old – eighty, ninety....

The fourth or fifth or sixth generation has already arrived, and that fifth or sixth generation cannot have any connection with a man one hundred and twenty years old, just vegetating in a hospital. Those new arrivals have no relationship, they don't have any respect.

Now, months pass and those old people are hanging around in the hospitals waiting, hoping that somebody may come – a friend, a child, an old acquaintance – to meet them. Nobody comes. People avoid them. They *are* boring, naturally. It is almost as if you are reading a fifty-year-old newspaper. They don't have anything new; everything is fifty, sixty years old. If you go to them they will talk only about those golden days when they used to be young, and life was an adventure. You cannot connect with them, and you feel simply bored. Everything has changed in fifty years, and those people are not even aware of what has changed.

But no government in the world accepts euthanasia, the right to die. In this long declaration it is not included.

Politicans are very, very cunning. They don't want to be controversial, so they say only things which you like or everybody is going to like. They are not concerned with the actual situation and the changes it needs. Their whole effort is in how to make you happy just by giving you bogus words.

Nowhere in the world are any of the basic rights being applied.

I will go through a few important rights.

Whereas disregard and contempt for human rights has resulted in barbarous acts which have outraged the conscience of mankind....

It has two implications in it. One is that the people who made this declaration have accepted that humanity is civilized. That's why once in a while if there is any barbarous act, those human beings in the world – the whole of mankind – suffers in conscience, feels the pain, the anguish. Both are lies, because I don't see humanity having any conscience.

When Mohammedans kill Hindus, no Mohammedan thinks that he has done wrong – the question of conscience does not arise. In fact, according to his religion he has done some virtuous act. He was trying to convert the Hindus to Mohammedanism, because if you are not a Mohammedan you cannot enter paradise. He was trying to help you in every possible way, to smuggle you, rightly or wrongly, into paradise – from the front door or the back door, it doesn't matter.

But you are resistant, you don't want to go to paradise, you are determined to go to hell – that's why he prevents you he beheads you – it is better to be killed by the hands of a religious Mohammedan. The *Koran* says, "The man who is killed by a Mohammedans will enter paradise, just as the Mohammedans who have killed him will enter paradise." So they are really trying to save people from going to hell – why should they feel any pain in their conscience?

No Hindu feels it, no Christian feels it. Christians have killed more people than anybody else, and particularly they have burned living people. Others have been killing and then burning; Christianity has a shortcut. Why make it in two parts? When the book can be published in one book, why make two volumes? First kill the man and then burn him? – burn him directly! Thousands of people have been burned alive.

I don't see anywhere that anybody is outraged.

If people are outraged things will change – because who is doing them? *We* are doing them.

This sentence in the beginning of the declaration is such a lie. First it says, *barbarous acts*....

In fact, in these fifty years we have done more barbarous acts than in the whole history of man. In ten thousand years we have not been able to do so many barbarous activities as we have done just within fifty years. We are becoming more and more barbarous – of course with a style and method.

Hiroshima and Nagasaki – what do you think? Are these barbarous acts, or an effort to send the beautiful people of Nagasaki and Hiroshima directly to paradise together? Whole cities, more than two hundred thousand people, entered within five minutes. I don't think there was ever such a crowd at the gates of paradise. And it was America that was responsible for Hiroshima and Nagasaki.

It is now absolutely confirmed by the people who understand military science that dropping the atom bombs on Hiroshima and Nagasaki was absolutely useless.

Japan was already surrendering – Germany had surrendered, and now there was no question that Japan could go on fighting; not for more than one week, or maybe not even that long.

Seeing that Germany was finished, Japan could not fight alone. It is a small country – of very courageous people, brave people, but a very small country. It was fighting with the support of Germany, and when the main support disappeared, Japan was going to surrender.

And this was the fear of President Truman of America: Japan may surrender tomorrow; then he will miss the chance to drop the atom bombs. And they had put so much money and energy and genius into creating atom bombs, they wanted to try them.

Man is not important, but money – their bombs had to be tried.

And you say that because of barbarous acts, the civilized people feel a prick of conscience. Was President Truman a civilized man or not? Even his own military experts had told him that it was absolutely meaningless, unnecessarily destroying human life. But he went ahead.

The next morning hundreds of journalists had gathered at the White House to see President Truman, because the world's greatest catastrophe created by man had happened. Their first question was, "Mr. President, did you have a good night's sleep?" – because he had gone to bed only after he had received the message: "Hiroshima and Nagasaki are in smoke, they are no longer on the map of the earth." Then he went to bed; otherwise he had waited for the news.

He said, "Yes, I slept more peacefully than ever, because our experiment has succeeded. Now we are the greatest power in the world."

And you are talking about conscience? More than two hundred thousand people died within three minutes, and the man whose order killed them, slept very "peacefully," as he had never slept before.

And if this is the situation of President 'True-man,' then what about the people who are not such true men?

As far as I am concerned, civilization is still a dream, a hope, a utopia. And if we don't get into the tricks of the magician and start believing that we are civilized people, the hope can become a reality, the dream can become a concrete experience.

And conscience arises only after meditation, never before it. You are not born with a conscience. You can watch small children: if they see an ant they will kill it. Do you think the small child has some conscience? Do you think the small child is a criminal, a murderer?

No, nothing like that. It is just out of curiosity, he's just exploring his world. He has entered into a new world, and he is exploring it. But there is no question of conscience. He does not feel that when he has been beating a dog for no reason, the dog also feels pain. Children don't have any conscience; they have only seeds.

All these politicians are trying to convince humanity: "You have a conscience." You *don't* have. You will have to grow it, you will have to work upon yourself. You will have to learn how to be silent, and how to listen to the still, small voice within.

I don't think any of the politicians who made this declaration have had any experience of what conscience is, of what consciousness is. It comes only after a long, long pilgrimage inwards.

You are not given everything by birth. You are given by birth only the necessary things for survival; everything else is given only as a seed. If you are intentionally interested in evolving your consciousness to its highest peak, then it is up to you.

Nature provides you only with survival – not life, not joy, not silence, not ecstasy, not love. Nature can manage itself with only lust – what is the need for love? Why create complications? Love you will have to find, consciousness you will have to grow. You will have to become a gardener of your own being – your being is your garden.

Your being is the Garden of Eden talked about in *The Bible*. That Garden of Eden is not somewhere else on some other star – it is within you. You have been thrown out of it, and you have been running all around but never going in. The moment you go in, you are back in the Garden of Eden. But now, nobody has taken care for thousands of years. You have never been back inside. Everything has gone to seed; now nothing blossoms, no foliage, no greenery. But you can bring it back to life because everything is potentially there.

These people don't understand what conscience is.

They have learned only words.

I have heard … a psychologist was appearing for an oral examination for his doctorate. There were three examiners. The first question they asked was: "What are the most important qualities of the human mother's milk?"

The psychologist was a little puzzled: "What has psychology to do with mother's milk? I have not come here to be an expert in milk products or anything. But what to do, I have to answer…. " So he said, "First, it has all the nutrients for the child's growth – it is perfect food. Second, it comes from within the mother's body, so it is warm, easily digestible; and because it comes from within, it cannot be carrying any infection, any disease which may be around. The child is protected."

They said, "Right! Now, the third?"

There was a moment of silence because he could not figure it out – what is the third? The first two also he had made up. The third was coming up again and again in his mind, but he was repressing it.

When he could not find anything else he had to say it. He said, "The third is that it comes in nice containers!"

Now, these idiots are going to be psychologists! And that was the first thing that had come to his mind – "nice containers."

Looking at the declaration, my first feeling was that these people are articulate, they can play with words. They can use beautiful words which influence you and deceive you, and hide the reality.

Article One: All human beings are born free...

This is absolutely nonsense.

If all human beings are born free, leave a child in freedom: he will die within twenty-four hours. Man's child is the most helpless child in the whole world – what freedom can he have? He cannot walk, he cannot talk, he cannot fly....

In fact, one scientist had the idea – and I feel some sympathy with his idea – that the human child is born earlier than he should be. He needs at least nine months more in the mother's womb because he is not complete, he's still growing. You see animals' kids – they are born and they start walking around and searching for food. They are more independent and they are more complete. For the human child it is impossible to survive without the support of the mother and the father and the family or other human beings.

What freedom can he have?

This is what I say is the most cunning part of the politician's mind: he is giving you the idea that you don't need freedom. "Don't ask for freedom, you are *born* free. All human beings are born free."

All human beings are born utterly helpless and dependent. It may take years for them to be free. Then too, millions of people never become free.

This declaration is saying that they are born free.

I am saying millions of people die – even then they are not free. And you know it from your life: you are not free.

The husband is there, the wife is not free. The wife is there, the husband is not free. I have seen husbands and wives walking on the road – the husband is not even free to look here and there! He looks straight ahead, like a Buddhist monk, just four feet ahead. And his wife is looking out of the corner of her eye – where is he? What kind of freedom is this?

The moment the husband reaches home, the first question is: "Where have you been?" – and you are a free man – "Why are you late?"

When I was in school, I was usually late.

Life outside was so beautiful, and around my school there were so many mango trees. And when the mango season comes, just to pass by the side of mango trees – such fragrance, such sweetness in the air. The mango is certainly the king of all the fruits. There were other fruit trees too, and I was mostly in those trees rather than in class.

On the first day when I reached middle school, I was half an hour late. The teacher said, "This won't do. At least with me, this will not do. If you have to study my subject, you have to be here before I come into the class – five minutes earlier. Why are you late?"

I said, "Listen – just because of this question I am not going to get married!"

He said, "What? ... the question of marriage?"

I said, "I will explain to you: I have been hearing it everywhere in my neighborhood; every wife is asking, 'Where have you been? Why are you late?' and I have decided that these questions I am not going to answer. So I am sacrificing my whole life, I'm not going to get married because of this question, and you think I will answer it for you? I would rather change the subject. Goodbye!"

He said to the class, "This is a strange boy. Irrelevant things he brings in – marriage? What has marriage to do with my subject, geography?"

But he became interested in me. After school he caught hold of me and he said, "Now we can sit. I want to understand what is the matter. Why?"

I said, "Nobody has the right to ask me why I am late, where I have been. It is *my* life; if I want to spoil it, it is my right. You are only a servant, to teach geography. You are not there to ask such questions to create dependence in me. I hate such questions.

"I can leave the school; I can completely forget about being educated. There is no need, because if Jesus, without being educated, can experience himself; if Kabir, without being educated, can know the ultimate.... I am not interested in any business, in any service, in any employment. So if you want me in your class, you will have to be a little more human – not continuously interfering in my freedom."

This first article says: *All human beings are born free.*

These are the strategies of hypnotizing and conditioning humanity.

They have given you the idea that you are *born* free – now there is no need to fight for freedom, there is no need to create an inner revolution which makes you *really* free – free from everything, free from the body … because the body is a bondage.

The East is far more truthful. It says you are born in bondage, not that you are born free. Your body is a prison and your mind and your brain are prisons. Your consciousness is confined in a very small space, and your consciousness is capable of spreading all over the universe. Because you don't know the potential, you think this is all you are.

These people, according to me, are criminals – greater criminals than those who go to the gallows – because they are deceiving the whole of humanity. But the deception is very clever: "You are born free." Naturally, freedom is not a question, not something to be created, to be deserved, to be earned, to be worthy of; you are already free!

George Gurdjieff is the only man in the whole of history who has said such a tremendously significant thing: "You don't have any soul."

Now, throughout the whole world all the religions believe that you have a soul, that you come with a soul. George Gurdjieff's voice is alone in the whole of history, saying that not all men have a soul; the place of the soul is empty. There is a possibility – you can work, you can create the soul – but you are not born with it.

I know, and Gurdjieff knows that you are born with a soul – but the idea that we are born with a soul has not been helpful. It has made man more asleep: We are born with a soul, God is within you, the kingdom of God is within you, so what do you have to do?

Things that are not within you, work hard to get them – money, power, respectability – because nobody says, "Every child is born with money, with political power, with respectability." Nobody will say that. These things have to be earned.

Freedom, consciousness, God, whatever you call it, has to be discovered. It is hidden, dormant; it has to be made dynamic, has to be made fully mature. It should be brought to flower and fruition.

But to tell people, "You are born free – *and equal in dignity and rights*"…. People can go on lying so smoothly, with such beautiful words – destroying those words.

Nobody is equal.

This is a psychological truth.

Neither in your body nor in your mind nor in your talents nor in your genius – nobody is equal. A Sigmund Freud is a Sigmund Freud; a Bertrand Russell is a Bertrand Russell; a D.H. Lawrence is a D.H. Lawrence. There is not even one other D.H. Lawrence, and never will be. Each individual is unique.

This idea of equality is so ugly, but it has become almost the religion of the contemporary man – "equality."

I say to you, it is the most destructive idea that has penetrated into the human mind. You have to be reminded about your uniqueness.

All human beings are endowed with reason and conscience and should act towards one another in a spirit of brotherhood.

These are all assumptions without any validity. All human beings are not born with reason, are not "endowed with reason." For example, there are people, very few ... I have just named Bertrand Russell – he can be said to be endowed with reason; J. Krishnamurti ... but ordinary people are living with all kinds of superstitions.

Unless you have dropped all your superstitions, you cannot be said to be a rational person. What does reason mean? For the Hindus, the cow is the mother. This is 'reason.'

I was talking to a *shankaracharya* – the equivalent of the pope to the Hindus.

I asked him, "Are you sure that the cow is your mother?"

He said, "What do you mean?"

"Now," I said, "just entering your temple, I met your mother. So I was puzzled: who is your mother, this woman or the cow? Or perhaps one is your stepmother?"

He said, "What are you talking about? The woman is my biological mother, but the cow is my spiritual mother."

I said, "My God! What about the bull? You must have some relationship with the bull or not? – your spiritual father? And who are you? – just a bull; or perhaps castrated, not even a bull."

You live with superstitions, and you talk about reason.

All Christians believe – and the whole group of politicians who have drawn up this declaration, ninety percent of them are Christians – they all believe that Jesus is born of a virgin mother. And they are rational beings....

It happened: One college girl got pregnant. She tried to hide it, but there are a few things you cannot hide. Truth is one, pregnancy is another! It is just impossible; it goes on becoming bigger and bigger.

Finally her mother discovered it. She said, "What is the matter?" And the girl had to confess.

The mother took her to the doctor. The doctor examined her and said, "Even without examining her I can see she is pregnant – and eight months. Now abortion is not possible."

The mother started shouting and screaming at the girl: "You have blackened our name, destroyed our respectability in the society."

But the girl said, "Mom, I have not even touched the hand of a man. How can I be pregnant? This is impossible!"

Hearing this, the doctor got out of his chair, went to the nearby window and looked at the sky. The mother said, "Why you are looking there?"

He said, "I am looking for the three wise men from the East."

She said, "What do you mean?"

He said, "And I am also looking for the star because it happened once – when Jesus was born. The star came, leading three wise men. It seems it has happened again – a virgin birth!"

But ask these Christians, "Where is your rationality?" Jesus is born out of virgin mother. He is crucified and he's resurrected too, he makes dead people come back to life – and these are the fundamentals on which the faith of a Christian depends.

You just take a few things out – it is very strange – and you will find Christianity to be the most irreligious religion, the poorest as far as religiousness is concerned.

The virgin birth – cancel it, if you have reason. Resurrection – cancel it, if you have reason. Walking on water – cancel it. Raising the dead back to life – cancel it. Changing water into alcohol – not only cancel it, but find the guy and give him to the police, because it is a crime, it is not a miracle. But if all these things are cancelled, what remains in Christianity? That is the poverty of Christianity.

In Buddhism, you cannot cancel anything because nothing is based on superstition. Buddha himself has cancelled anything that smells of superstition – it is just pure rationality.

But to say that man is endowed with reason by birth.... It doesn't seem so. Looking at the world, it doesn't seem that it is a rational world. We have not been living according to reason, we have been living according to all kinds of irrational things.

But these are sweet words to believe: that you are *endowed with reason.* The more idiotic you are, the more you will believe it, and sooner.

... and conscience, and should act towards one another in a spirit of brotherhood.

Conscience arises only after deep meditation – never before it. It is a flowering of meditation.

Only very few people in the whole world, in the whole of history, have been conscious, have had conscience. Both the words mean the same, but because of religious people, in all the languages except French they have created different meanings for the two words. Only in French is 'conscience' and 'consciousness' one word, it means the same thing.

Religions around the world have tried to take conscience separately from consciousness for a certain reason: consciousness comes only after meditation. How long can you deceive people?

It is just like when you bring light into the room, and darkness disappears. The moment you are in a meditative state, you have consciousness, awareness.

They created another word, 'conscience.' And conscience is what the priests, the church, the religion, teach you about what is good, what is bad, what is virtuous, what is sin – all these teachings make your conscience. It is a very clever trick to separate conscience from consciousness. There can be no conscience without consciousness. But they have created a false, artificial conscience.

For example, I was born in a very ancient religion – perhaps the ancientmost. It is a small religion as far as numbers are concerned, but they have their superstitions.

Up to the age of eighteen I had not seen a tomato in my house. Do you think tomatoes are dangerous people? But because the color of the tomato is the color of meat, that was enough to debar it. Up to the age of eighteen I had never eaten in the night, because it is prohibited by that religion – you can eat only between sunrise and sunset. Eating in the night you may eat some insect, some ant; some violence may happen. So it is better to eat in light, in full light.

When I was eighteen my friends were going to see a beautiful castle very close by, a few miles away. I went with them. I had no idea, I had not even thought about it, but going up the hill to the castle ... and it was so beautiful, so old, and there were so many things to see, that nobody was ready to prepare food.

I asked, "Do something – soon the sun will be setting and I am feeling very hungry, you are feeling hungry. The whole day long we have been moving on the mountain ... it has been tiring, but it has been an experience."

They said, "As long as the sun is there, we don't want to miss. There are a few more things to see."

I was the only one who was not accustomed to eating in the night. They were all eating at night so there was no question. By nine or ten o'clock in the night, they had prepared such delicious food – and particularly after the whole day's hunger, starvation, and moving on the mountain, I was in a dilemma – what to do?

Then I told them: "There is a great difficulty. I have never eaten in the night, and the religion in which unfortunately I have been born, thinks that if you eat in the night, you will go to hell. I don't want to go to hell just for one night's food, but I cannot sleep either. Moreover, the smell of your food is too much!"

They persuaded me, saying, "We will not tell your parents or anybody. Nobody will ever know that you have eaten in the night."

I said, "That is not the point – *I* will know. The question is not my parents or anybody. You can tell the whole world, that's not the problem. The problem is that I cannot conceive of myself eating at night, after eighteen years of continuous conditioning."

But they persuaded me – and I had to be persuaded.

I ate, but I could not sleep; I had to vomit the whole night. Now, nobody else vomited. Twenty persons were with me; they all slept – they were tired, they had eaten good food. They slept well. I had to remain awake the whole night, vomiting. Unless I was completely clean of the food, I could not sleep. It was just in the morning near-about five that I went to sleep.

That gave me the idea: perhaps eating in the night *is* dangerous. Just one time and the whole night became hell! And those who have been eating in the night for their whole lives ... perhaps the idea that they go to hell is right.

But the whole world is eating in the night. If it is true, then everybody will be going to hell. And these twenty friends are sleeping so beautifully – nobody has vomited so nothing was wrong with the food, and nothing is wrong with these people. Something is wrong in my conditioning; I have been brought up with a wrong idea.

But once you accept something, this creates a false conscience that goes on telling you, "Don't do this, do this."

This is not consciousness.

Consciousness simply *knows* what to do, what not to do. There is no question of choice. Consciousness is a choiceless state – you simply know what is right.

You are not born with conscience. It has been created by the religions, and they have exploited man through creating conscience. It is time that we should drop the word 'conscience' because it has become associated with a long past and has wrong connotations.

You should use the word 'consciousness.'

But consciousness is the fragrance of your becoming absolutely silent; it does not come with your birth. Yes, if you can attain consciousness, you will have a new birth; you will be reborn.

That's what Jesus meant when he said to Nicodemus, "Unless you are born again, you will not understand me." He does not mean in your next life. He means "You will have to transform your being, rise in your consciousness. Only then will you be able to understand me."

If you have consciousness and silence and meditativeness, there is no need to say that the whole of humanity is one. It *is* – it is your experience.

And it will not be only a brotherhood, it will be a brotherhood and a sisterhood! But it will be just a byproduct; there is no need to declare it as a fundamental right.

Article Two: Everyone is entitled to all the rights and freedoms set forth in this Declaration without distinction of any kind, such as race, color, sex, language, religion, political or other opinion, national or social origin, property, birth or other status.

All these are bullshit.

The first question I was asked as I entered America was that I had to declare under oath that I am not an anarchist. If I am an anarchist, I cannot enter America. Anarchism is a political ideology.

I cannot conceive that these people go on declaring these things. Who is going to ask them: "When are you going to practice them?" Everywhere there is discrimination – in different ways in different countries, but discrimination is there.

Mankind needs a great uproar against these so-called humanitarians. They think they are doing a great service.

For example, in India, for the same amount of work the woman will be paid less. And in this declaration it is said that for the same amount of labor, the same rewards should be paid – whether it is man or woman, white or black does not matter. But it is not true.

In America, I was in six jails, and in all the jails there was not a single white man. In six federal jails – which were huge, six hundred people, seven hundred people in one jail ... but all black people. And you say discrimination is not there. It seems strange – in a white country all the criminals are black.

And that was not all. I inquired of a few black inmates – because they all loved me; they had been watching me on television every day for five years, and they had become involved in controversies themselves. They were reading my books, and they were happy that I had come at least for one day to their jail – they would remember this day for their whole lives. I asked them, "What is your crime?"

They said, "All these people you see have not committed any crime. They have been arrested the way you have been arrested – without any arrest warrant. And we have been told again and again: 'You will be taken to the court next week, tomorrow,' but that tomorrow never comes." One man told me that he had been there for nine months without being taken to court.

Now this declaration says nobody should be arrested without an arrest warrant, nobody should be kept in jail unless he is proved a criminal. Innocence needs no proof; you have to prove a person criminal, only then can you keep him in jail. Otherwise you cannot keep him in jail. But people have been there for nine months, eight months, six months in jail – and all young people.

So I started figuring out the reason: it is not that they have done anything wrong. The reason is that they are young and revolutionaries. They want rights for the blacks, equal rights for blacks. That is their crime. But they cannot be taken to court because the court will release them, so they go on keeping them in jail. But this is absolutely criminal on the part of the government of the U.S.

I have seen only six jails and near about three or four thousand young black people. Perhaps thousands of people are in other jails. They told me, "There is too much pressure from all over the world, that's why they are taking you to court. Otherwise, if the world had remained silent, if the news media had not spread all over the world that the whole government is doing everything criminal against an innocent person.... The pressure is too much and the eyes of the whole news media are focused on you. They are, under compulsion, reluctantly, taking you to court."

Still, they took twelve days. That too is against human rights. From the place where I was arrested, the court where I had to be present was only a five-hour flight. My own jet was there. We offered them our jet; we said, "You can have your pilots; you can have your people, and you can take me to the court. What is the need to keep me here in your jail?" They would only take me in their own airplane.

The whole strategy was: "Today the airplane has not come ... something is wrong with the airplane." They had only one airplane, it seems. "The pilot is sick... "

They took twelve days to make a five-hour journey. But looking at other inmates I thought, "It is very quick, only twelve days.... "

Every government goes on doing everything illegal and everything against human rights. And these people are the representatives of governments and without any shame they can make this declaration – perhaps without even feeling what they are doing. They are lying utterly – white lies!

Article Three: Everyone has the right to life, liberty and security of person.

But death is not included – and it is important. Because birth is not in your hands – you are born without your consent – now only death is there. And you have the choice: either to die without your consent or to die with a dignity of a human being, with your own consent – not to give death a chance, but to move, yourself, when you have lived.

But they are worried about putting death into it because then all the religions and all the political parties will be creating havoc for them. Everything has to be consolatory: 'life' – but what kind of life?

Just in the last year, six months ago, in Europe the common market had accumulated mountains of butter and other foodstuffs. People were dying in Ethiopia – one thousand people per day – and they had a surplus but they would not give it to Ethiopia.

That surplus had to be drowned in the ocean.

Just in drowning it, two billion dollars were wasted – that was not the value of the food, it was just the labor of shifting and drowning it in the ocean. And they are doing it every six months, because every six months the surplus is there and you need more warehouses. And what will you do with it? – fresh crops are coming. But you will not give it to Ethiopa.

In India, fifty percent of the people are living below the medical standard of nourishment and twenty-five percent of the people are almost starving. Fifty percent of people in the villages are eating only one time a day – and when I say eating, don't think of the Taj Mahal Hotel. It means just bread, salt, a little sauce from mangoes or from other fruits – that's all. This is not food.

Unless the world is one, we will not be able to give everybody enough nourishment.

And what does it mean to say that you have the right to life? Because people *are* there; and people are dying, people have died. America is doing the same, Stalin's Russia was doing the same.

It is not something happening only in Europe. Every three months America drowns its surplus – and that is worth billions of dollars. In the days of Stalin, Russia was using wheat instead of coal in their railway trains because wheat is cheaper, it is surplus and coal is difficult and costly to obtain in Russia.

People are dying – that is not important.

People are starving – that is not important.

Article Nine: No one shall be subjected to arbitrary arrest, detention or exile.

I have been subjected, so I am a witness to it, that this declaration is not being used by any government – and particularly by America, which was the sponsor for this declaration.

I have been in detention in England – not even for an *arbitrary* reason. I wanted just to stay for six hours at the airport in the first-class lounge because my pilots had flown their time and they wanted to rest. It is against their laws to fly more than twelve hours, so we had to stop.

My pilots said, "They may create trouble; they may say that the first-class lounge is for first-class passengers and you are not a passenger; you have your own plane. Now what class is it, how can they decide?"

So I told my people to purchase two tickets, two first-class tickets for the morning flight: "We will go with our plane, but purchase two tickets in case they bring up this point" – and they brought up that point. Then we brought up the tickets!

The officer was shocked. He had not thought that we would have tickets too. I said, "Now what do you think?"

He said, "I cannot do anything. I will have to ask the higher authorities."

And who was the higher authority? It seems it was the prime minister herself. When the man was gone I looked into his file; he had left it on the table. The government had given him orders.

I have never asked for any entry visa into England. They should not have bothered. But they decided in Parliament that I should not be allowed in the country – in case I should ask to enter.

When the man came back I told him, "I do not *want* to enter England. Even if the whole of England wants me to enter England, I am the last person to do it. I have no business in England, I just want to sleep in the lounge. And from the lounge you cannot enter the country. It is closed; you will remain only at the airport. And the airport is international, it is not England."

But he said, "What can I do? The insistence is from the top: 'If he insists then put him in detention. That's the only way. He can remain in jail for six hours.' "

I had to remain in jail for six hours – not even for an arbitrary reason. I had not committed any crime, I had the tickets, I had the plane, I just wanted to rest.

But the politicians – because I have been exposing them continuously – now have become so frightened that even my sleeping six hours in the lounge at the airport is dangerous for the religion of England, its morality, its character. I can corrupt the youth just by staying in the lounge!

These people are not lovers of human beings.

Nor do they have any respect for human dignity.

Article Eighteen: Everyone has the right to freedom of thought, conscience and religion; this right includes freedom to change his religion or belief, and freedom, either alone or in community with others and in public or private, to manifest his religion or belief in teaching, practice, worship and observance.

"Freedom of thought and expression" – I have never done anything except to express my thoughts. If that is a human right, then no government has anything against me.

I am not active in any politics; I am not interested in any power.

I am simply saying whatsoever I see more clearly than all these blind politicians.

What is the fear?

Just now the pope has called a World Conference of Religions. All the chief priests and leaders of other religions have been called.

My sannyasins from Italy have been writing to me: "We are insisting to the pope – and his secretary is very much interested in you and is willing to extend an invitation, but the pope is against it."

In fact for eight months the Italian government has been thinking about whether to give me a three weeks' tourist visa or not. And the pope has been the cause of the whole delay.

And these people go on saying, "We love freedom of thought, freedom of expression."

Nobody loves freedom of thought. It has to support *him,* then it is loved.

"Freedom of expression...."

The pope has put my books on the black list so that no Catholic should read them. They have a black list, and in the Middle Ages, whenever a book appeared on the black list it was burned all over Europe.

Now they cannot do that, but this much they can do: no Catholic should read it. And Catholics are not a small minority – seven hundred million people, a world in itself. Now, preventing them simply means you have accepted defeat; it simply means you don't have any answers to me.

But then why all this nonsense about a Declaration of Human Rights?

Article Nineteen: Everyone has the right to freedom of opinion and expression; this right includes freedom to hold opinions without inter ference and to seek, receive and impart information and ideas through any media and regardless of frontiers.

This is not right. The Indian parliament has urged Indian journalists and news media people not to give any space to my ideas.

The American government has been pressuring the Indian government so that no news media people from the West should be allowed to take my interview.

The American government has been doing two things: telling all the governments of Europe, and Australia, that I should not be allowed to reside in their countries, that I should be sent back from everywhere to India.

So all the countries of Europe have passed resolutions in their parliaments that I cannot be allowed in their country even as a tourist for three weeks.

The American idea is that I should not be allowed to enter any other country and nobody who wants to see me or meet me should be allowed to come to India. In this way they feel they can destroy the sannyas movement.

This goes on in reality. And in words, beautiful and great slogans ... but empty.

Article Twenty-two: Everyone has the right to the free development of his personality.

I don't see that you are allowed to have freedom to develop your personality. In the first place, the people who wrote this don't know that personality is the false part of you, and it has not to be developed at all.

Your reality is your individuality, which has to be discovered. But they don't talk about individuality.

They may not have ever thought of it. Because they are only personalities, they don't yet have their individuality awake, alert. Naturally, they are writing the word 'personality.'

'Personality' is an ugly word.

It means a mask; the very root of the word is 'mask.' And we don't want people to have masks.

People should be natural, spontaneous, themselves.

Article Twenty-five: All children, whether born in or out of wedlock, shall enjoy the same social protection.

Now, if this is true, it cancels marriage! If a child born from a marriage and a child born outside of marriage have the same rights, then marriage loses all meaning. What is the meaning of marriage? But they don't have the courage to say that.

And this too is not true, because nowhere are children born outside marriage respected. They are condemned in every possible way.

I gave this much time to this rubbish because these are the people who are controlling the whole world, and these are the people whose heads should be hammered as much as possible. They have kept humanity in slavery – this should not be allowed anymore.

They don't have any right of declaration.

We have the right to declare.

We are the people.

As far as my people are concerned, we declare that we will live freedom, love, humanity. We will grow into our individuality and we will help anybody who is inviting and welcoming us.

The only basic right is to become god.

And unless you have found god within yourself, everything else is mundane. Finding godliness within you, everything else is found simultaneously.

"Beloved Bhagwan,

On December 25, You spoke to us on the Declaration of Human Rights. You exposed it as a political device to maintain man in his current state of physical and psychological slavery, and to ensure that he remains ignorant of his true potential for godliness.

Would You, tonight, make Your own Declaration of Human Rights for the new man?"

The Declaration of Human Rights basically means that mankind still lives in many kinds of slaveries. Otherwise, there would be no need for the declaration.

The very need indicates that man has been deceived for thousands of years. And he has been deceived in such a cunning way that unless you rise above humanity, you cannot see in what invisible chains humanity is living, in what bondage, in what invisible prisons everybody is confined.

My declaration of human rights consists of ten fundamental things.

The first is life.

Man has a right to dignity, to health; a right to grow so that he can blossom into his ultimate flowering. This ultimate flowering is his right. He is born with the seeds, but the society does not provide him the soil, the right caring, the loving atmosphere.

On the contrary, society provides a very poisonous atmosphere, full of anger, hatred, destruction, violence, war. The right to life means there should be no wars anymore. It also means that nobody should be forced into armies, forced to go to war; it is everybody's right to refuse. But this is not the case.

Thousands of people are in prisons – particularly young people, sensitive and intelligent – because they refused to go to war. Their denial has become a crime – and they were simply saying that they don't want to kill human beings.

Human beings are not things you can destroy without a second thought. They are the climax of universal evolution. To destroy them for any cause – for religion, for politics, for socialism, for fascism … it does not matter what the cause is; man is above all causes, and man cannot be sacrificed on any altar.

It is so strange that the U.N. declares the fundamental rights of human beings and yet says nothing about those thousands of young people who are wasting their lives in prisons for the simple reason that they refused to destroy life. But it has deep roots which have to be understood.

The right to life is possible only in a certain different atmosphere which is not present on the earth at the moment. Animals are killed, birds are killed, sea animals are killed, just as a game. You don't have any reverence for life. And life is the same whether it is in human beings or in other forms. Unless man becomes aware of his violence towards animals, birds, he cannot be really alert about his own right to life. If you are not caring about others' lives, what right have you got to demand the same right for yourself?

People go hunting, killing animals unnecessarily. I was a guest in Maharaja Jamnagar's palace. He showed me hundreds of lions, deer – their heads. The whole palace was full, and he was showing them: "These are the animals I have killed myself."

I asked him, "You look a nice a person. What was the reason? What have these animals done against you?"

He said, "It is not a question of reason or a question of them doing anything against me. It is just a game."

I said, "Just look from the other side: If a lion killed you, would that be a game? Your wife, your children, your brothers – will any one of them have the guts to say that it was a beautiful game? It will be a disaster. If *you* kill, then it is a game; if they kill, then it is a calamity. These double standards show your dishonesty, insincerity."

He said, "I have never thought about it."

But the whole of humanity is non-vegetarian; they are all eating other life forms. There is no reverence for life as such. Unless we create an atmosphere of reverence for life, man cannot realize the goal of getting his fundamental right of life.

Secondly, because the U.N. also declares life to be a fundamental right for man, it is being misused. The pope, Mother Teresa and their tribe are using it for teaching people against birth control, against abortion, against the pill. Man's mind is so cunning.

It was a question of human rights – they are taking advantage of it. They are saying you cannot use birth control methods because they go against life; the unborn child also has the same right as you have. So some line has to be drawn, because at what point… ?

To me, the pill does not destroy human rights; in fact it prepares the ground for it. If the earth is too overcrowded, millions of people will die of starvation; there will be wars. And the way the crowd is exploding it can lead humanity into a very inhuman situation.

In Bengal, there was a great famine in which mothers ate their own children. People sold their own children just for one rupee, two rupees. And do you think the persons who were purchasing them were purchasing human beings? No, they were purchasing food.

The pope and Mother Teresa will be responsible for all this.

The pill simply does not allow the child to be formed in the mother's womb, so the question of human rights does not arise. And now, recently, science has found a pill for men too. It is not necessary that the woman should take the pill, the man can take it. The child is not formed in any way; hence, this fundamental right is inapplicable in that case. But these religious people – the *shankaracharyas* in India, Ayatollah Khomeini in Iran … and all over the world, all religions are against birth control methods. And they are the only methods which can prevent man from falling into a barbarous state.

I am absolutely in favor of birth control methods. A child should be recognized as a human being when he is born – and then too, I have some reservations…. If a child is born blind, if a child is born crippled, if a child is born deaf, dumb, and we cannot do anything…. Just because life should not be destroyed, this child will have to suffer – because of your stupid idea – for seventy years, eighty years. Why create unnecessary suffering? If the parents are willing, the child should be put to eternal sleep. And there is no problem in it. Only the body goes back into its basic elements; the soul will fly into another womb. Nothing is destroyed.

If you really love the child, you will not want him to live a seventy-year-long life in misery, suffering, sickness, old age. So even if a child is born, if he is not medically capable of enjoying life fully with all the senses, healthy, then it is better that he goes to eternal sleep and is born somewhere else with a better body.

The right to life is a complex thing. Nobody is entitled to kill anyone, either, in the name of religion. Millions of people have been killed in the name of religions, in the service of God.

No one should be killed in the name of politics. Again, the same has happened. Joseph Stalin alone killed one million people, his own people, while he was in power. Adolf Hitler killed six million people. And thousands of wars have happened.

It seems that on this earth we are doing only one thing: reproducing children because soldiers are needed, reproducing children because wars are needed. Even to increase the population, Mohammed said that every Mohammedan can marry four women or even more. He himself married nine women. And the reason is war, destruction of life. It is not out of love for nine women that he has married them, it is simple arithmetic. If a man marries nine women, he can produce nine children in one year. If nine women marry one man, this is okay but vice-versa, nine men marrying one woman may not be able even to produce one child. They will mess up the whole thing. Most probably they will kill the woman!

It seems man is nothing but a necessary instrument for more destruction, more wars.

The population has to be reduced if man wants to be, to have his dignity, honor, his right to live – not just to drag, but to dance. When I say life is a fundamental right, I mean a life of songs and dances, a life of joy and blessings.

My second consideration is for love.

Love should be accepted as one of the most fundamental human rights, and all societies have destroyed it. They have destroyed it by creating marriage. Marriage is a false substitute for love.

In the past, small children were married. They had no idea what love is, what marriage is. And why were small children married? For a simple reason: before they become young adults, before love arises in their hearts, the doors have to be closed. Because once love takes possession of their hearts then it will become very difficult....

No child marriage is human. A man or a woman should be allowed to choose their partners and to change their partners whenever they feel. The government has no business in it, the society has nothing to do with it. It is two individuals' personal affair. The privacy of it is sacred.

If two people want to live together, they don't need any permission from any priest or any government. They need the permission of their hearts. And the day they feel that the time has come to part, again they don't need anybody's permission. They can part as friends, with beautiful memories of their loving days.

Love should be the only way for men and women to live together. No other ritual is needed.

The only problem in the past was what would happen to the children; that was the argument for marriage. There are other alternatives, far better. Children should be accepted not as their parents' property – they belong to the whole humanity. From the very beginning it should be made clear to them: "The whole humanity is going to protect you, is your shelter. We may be together – we will look after you. We may not be together; still we look after you. You are our blood, our bones, our souls."

In fact, this possession by the parents of the children is one of the most dangerous things that humanity goes on carrying. This is the root of the idea of possessiveness. You should not possess your children. You can love them, you can bless them, but you cannot possess them. They belong to the whole humanity. They come from beyond; you have been just a passage. Don't think more than that about yourself. Whatever you can do, do.

Every commune, every village should take care of the children. Once the commune starts taking care of the children, marriage becomes absolutely obsolete. And marriage is destroying your basic right to love.

If man's love is free, there will not be blacks and whites, and there will not be these ugly discriminations, because love knows no boundaries. You can fall in love with a black man, you can fall in love with a white man.

Love knows no religious scriptures. It knows only the heartbeat, and it knows it with absolute certainty. Once love is free, it will prepare the ground for other fundamental rights.

In fact, if you ask the scientists, people falling in love should be as different as possible. Then they will give birth to better children, more intelligent, stronger. We know it now; we are trying it all over the world as far as animals are concerned. Crossbreeding has given us better cows, better horses, better dogs. But man is strange. You know the secret, but you are not bettering yourself.

All the royal families are suffering. They create the greatest number of idiots, because they go on marrying amongst themselves. Royal blood cannot mix with a commoner's blood – even in the twentieth century we think in terms of royal blood. Blood is simply blood. But if just a dozen families go on marrying amongst themselves contintually, they create many kinds of diseases.

Retardedness is one. Just have a look again at the picture of the Prince of Wales and you will see what I mean by a retarded person. They are fed up, but they cannot go out of their small circle. I have never come across any person belonging to a royal family who has intelligence, and in India I have been acquainted with almost all the royal families. It is not only that their minds remain retarded, their bodies lose many things.

You must have heard the name of Rasputin. Before the Russian revolution he had become the most important man in Russia, for the simple reason that the child of the czar had a disease – if he wounded himself accidentally then the bleeding could not be prevented. No medicine could prevent it, there was no way; the blood would go on flowing out. And that is one of the symptoms of marrying close relatives.

Rasputin was a great hypnotist. He was not a saint and he was not a sinner, he was simply a great hypnotist. He managed with hypnosis to prevent the blood from flowing out of the child. What no physician was able to do ... and the child was going to be the successor to the greatest empire of those days. Rasputin certainly became very important. Without him the child's life was in danger.

But still those royal families, although they have lost their kingdoms, their empires, continue to marry amongst themselves. It creates a very weak personality. Have you ever seen somebody from these royal families being declared as the beauty queen of the world? Do you think Queen Elizabeth of England can even be declared a beauty? All over England there is a rumor...I don't know whether it is true or not; hence I don't take any responsibility for it. The rumor is that Prince Philip, the husband of Queen Elizabeth, is a homosexual. I feel sorry for poor Philip. In fact anybody marrying Elizabeth would have been homosexual, so he should not feel worried about it. It is just natural.

And just two weeks or three weeks ago, one of the bodyguards of Prince Charles died of the disease AIDS. Now you cannot get AIDS from the sky. One does not know who the holy ghost is, but he must be in the royal family. And soon many more will die, because it is a chain disease.

There should be no boundaries – that a Hindu should marry only a Hindu, or a brahmin should only marry a brahmin. In fact, the rule should be that the Indian should never marry an Indian. The whole world is there; find your spouse far away, beyond the seven seas.

Then you will have children who are more beautiful, more healthy, longer living, far more intelligent, geniuses. Man has to learn crossbreeding, but that is possible only if marriage disappears and love is given absolute respect. Right now it is condemned.

The third most fundamental right ... because these are the three most important things in life: life, love, and death. Everybody should be given the fundamental right that after a certain age, when he has lived enough and does not want to go on dragging unnecessarily – because tomorrow will be again just a repetition; he has lost all curiosity about tomorrow – he has every right to leave the body. It is his fundamental right.

It is his life. If he does not want to continue, nobody should prevent him. In fact, every hospital should have a special ward where people who want to die can enter one month before, can relax, enjoy all the things that they have been thinking about their whole life but could not manage – the music, the literature ... if they wanted to paint or sculpt....

And the doctors should take care to teach them how to relax. Up to now, death has been almost ugly. Man has been a victim, but it is our fault. Death can be made a celebration; you just have to learn how to welcome it, relaxed, peaceful. And in one month's time, people, friends, can come to see them and meet together. Every hospital should have special facilities – more facilities for those who are going to die than for those who are going to live. Let them live for one month at least like emperors, so they can leave life with no grudge, with no complaint but only with deep gratitude, thankfulness.

Among these three comes the fourth: the search for truth.

Nobody should be conditioned from childhood about any religion, any philosophy, any theology, because you are destroying his freedom to search. Help him to be strong enough. Help him to be strong enough to doubt, to be skeptical about all that is believed all around him. Help him never to believe, but to insist on knowing. And whatever it takes, however long it takes, to go for the pilgrimage alone, on his own, because there is no other way to find the truth.

All others – who think they are Christians, who think they are Jews, who think they are Hindus, who think they are Mohammedans – these are all believers. They don't *know*.

Belief is pure poison.

Knowing is coming to a flowering.

The search for truth ... you should not teach anybody what truth is because it cannot be taught. You should help the person to inquire. Inquiry is difficult; belief is cheap. But truth is not cheap; truth is the most valuable thing in the world. You cannot get it from others, you will have to find it yourself.

And the miracle is, the moment you decide that "I will not fall victim to any belief," you have already travelled half the way towards truth.

If your determination is total, you need not go to truth, truth will come to you. You just have to be silent enough to receive it. You have to become a host so that truth can become a guest in your heart.

Right now the whole world is living in beliefs. That's why there is no shine in the eyes, no grace in people's gestures, no strength, no authority in their words. Belief is bogus; it is making castles of sand. A little breeze and your great castle will be destroyed.

Truth is eternal, and to find it means you also become part of eternity.

Fifth: to find the truth, all education systems from the kindergarten to the universities will create a certain atmosphere for meditation. Meditation does not belong to any religion, and meditation is not a belief. It is a pure science of the inner.

Learning to be silent, learning to be watchful, learning to be a witness; learning that you are not the mind, but something beyond – the consciousness – will prepare you to receive truth.

And it is truth that has been called by many people, "God," by others, "nirvana." By others, other names have been given to it, but it is a nameless silence, serenity, peace. The peace is so deep that you disappear; and the moment you disappear you have entered the temple of God.

But strange it is, that people are wasting almost one-third of their lives in schools, colleges, and universities, not knowing anything about silence, not knowing anything about relaxation, not knowing anything about themselves. They know about the whole world – it is very weird that they have forgotten only themselves. But it seems there is some reason....

In India there is an ancient story. Ten blind men pass through a stream. The current is very forceful, so they hold hands. Reaching the other side, somebody suggests, "We should count ourselves. The current was so forceful and we cannot see – somebody may have gone with the wind, gone with the river."

So they count. Strangely enough the counting always stops at nine. Everybody tries, but it is always nine. One man sitting on the bank of the river starts laughing – it is hilarious! And those ten blind people are sitting there crying, tears in their eyes because they have lost one of their friends.

The man comes to them and he says, "What is the matter?"

They explain the situation. He says, "You all stand up in a line. I will hit the first person – he has to say 'one.' I will hit the second person – he has to say 'two,' because I will hit twice. I will hit the third person three times; he has to say 'three.'"

Strangely enough, he finds the tenth man who was lost. They all thank him, they touch his feet; they say, "You are a god to us. We were thinking we had lost one of our friends. But please, can you tell us … we were also counting; all of us tried, and the tenth was not there. How has he appeared suddenly?"

The man says, "That is an ancient mystery which you will not understand. You just go on your way."

What is the ancient mystery in it? One tends to forget oneself. In fact, one lives his whole life without remembering himself. He sees everybody, he knows everybody; he just forgets himself.

Meditation is the only method in which you will start counting from yourself: "one."

And because it is not part of any religion, there is no problem – it should be all over the world, in every school, in every college, in every university. Anybody who comes home from the university should come with a deep, meditative being, with an aura of meditation around him. Otherwise, what he is bringing is all rubbish, crap. Geography he knows: he knows where Timbuktu is, he knows where Constantinople is, and he does not know where he is himself.

The first thing in life is to know who you are, where you are. Then everything in your life starts settling, moving in the right direction.

The sixth: freedom in all dimensions.

We are not even as free as birds and animals. No bird goes to the passport office. Any moment he can fly into Pakistan; no entry visa. Strange, that only man remains confined in nations, in boundaries. Because the nation is big, you tend to forget that you are imprisoned. You cannot get out of it, you cannot get into it. It is a big prison, and the whole earth is full of big prisons.

Freedom in all dimensions means that man, wherever he is born, is part of one humanity.

Nations should dissolve, religions should dissolve, because they are all creating bondages – and sometimes very hilarious bondages.

I was in a city, Devas. For twenty years the Jaina temple there has not opened. There are three locks on the temple: one lock from the *Digambaras,* one of the sects of Jainism, one from another sect, *Svetambaras,* and the third from the police. For twenty years poor Mahavira has been inside – no food, no bath, no light. One wonders whether he is really alive or dead, because he does not make any noise ... at least he could knock and shout, "Open the doors and let me out!"

When I saw it, I asked, "What is the matter?" I was just passing by and I saw three locks – big locks, bigger than you may have ever seen – and I came to know the story.

In Devas, there is only one Jaina temple, and this was the temple. Jainas are few; they don't have enough money to make two temples, so they have made one temple and divided the time. Up to twelve o'clock in the morning, Digambaras will worship, and after twelve, Svetambaras will worship ... but there was a fight every day.

The differences between Svetambaras and Digambaras are not very big – so childish and so stupid. Digambaras worship Mahavira with closed eyes and Svetambaras worship Mahavira with open eyes. This is the only basic difference.

Now a marble statue ... either you can make the eyes closed or you can make the eyes open, unless you fix some mechanism, to switch on so he opens his eyes, and switch off.... But that much technology does not exist in India; otherwise it would not be difficult. You can find it in toys – a beautiful girl, you lie her down and she closes her eyes. You put her back and she opens her eyes. Something could have been arranged.

They had something arranged – primitive, but they had arranged it. It is being followed all over India: When Svetambaras worship a statue which has closed eyes, they put false eyes on top; they just glue them on. That is simple, non-technical; not much technology is needed. But every day the problem was there: at the time of twelve, exactly twelve, Svetambaras would be waiting. One minute more ... and the Digambaras are worshipping – and they are worshipping a little longer *knowingly* – and the Svetambaras will come and start putting their eyes on the statue and the fight will start.

It happened so many times that finally the police locked the temple and said to them, "Go to the court and get a decision."

The case goes on – how can the court decide whether Mahavira used to meditate with closed eyes or with open eyes? The reality is, he used to meditate with half open eyes.

No child should be given any idea by the parents what life is all about – no theology, no philosophy, no politics. He should be made as intelligent and sharp as possible, so when he comes of age he can go in search. And it is a lifelong search. People today get their religion when they are born. In fact, if you can get your religion when you die, you have found it early. It is such a precious treasure, but it is possible only out of freedom – and freedom in all dimensions, not only in religion.

There should be no nations, no national boundaries. There should be no religions. Man should be taken as man. Why confine him with so many adjectives? Right now he is not free in any way.

I was arrested in America. In one jail in Oklahoma, the U.S. Marshal told me that I had to write my name as David Washington. I said, "This is the first time that somebody has told me my name. Do you read thoughts?"

He became a little puzzled. He said, "Is it really your name?"

I said, "Of course."

He said, "Then change it. Some other name will do."

But I said, "You know my name. David Washington is not my name. And why should I write David Washington? And you call this country a democracy! – and not even the freedom to write one's own name! What other freedoms do you have? And on your coat there is written in big letters 'Department of Justice, U.S. Marshal.' " I said, "At least take this coat off. David Washington is not my name and I am not going to write it." I said, "This is for the first time in my life that I am seeing how democracy works, how freedom works. I am not even free to write my name. What is the purpose?"

He said, "That, I don't know. From high above I have been ordered: 'David Washington should be his name and he should be called David Washington in jail.' "

I said, "Then you fill out the form" – and it was in the middle of the night, twelve o'clock. I said, "You fill out the form – I will not fill it out, I refuse – and then I will sign it."

He was in a hurry to go home, so he filled out the form. I signed *my* name. He looked at it and he said, "But it doesn't look like David Washington."

I said, "How can it? *I* don't look like David Washington."

He said, "You are a strange man. You deceived me."

I said, "You are deceiving yourself. You know perfectly well what my name is. And tomorrow the whole world will know that the so-called democracies – free countries, talking too much of freedom – are not even able to allow people to write their own names." And I said, "You don't know the reason why your higher authorities have asked this?"

He said, "I don't know."

I said, "This is strange, because I know. It is a simple, logical inference that even if you kill me in the jail nobody will be able to find out where I disappeared. Because in your forms, on your register, I never entered your jail, so the question of my being killed in your jail does not arise."

He was shocked. I said, "This is a simple thing. Otherwise, there is no need to change my name; you don't have any authority."

But in this world there is no freedom in any dimension.

I was going to college. My parents wanted me to go to science college or to medical college. I said, "Am I going or are you going?"

They said, "Of course you are going; why should we be going?"

"Then," I said, "leave it to me."

They said, "We can leave it to you, but then remember: we will not support you financially."

I said, "That's understood." I left my home without a single rupee. I traveled in the train to the university without a ticket. I had to go to the ticket checker and tell him: "This is the situation. Can you allow me to travel without a ticket?"

He said, "This is the first time in my life that somebody has come to ask me! People escape, people deceive me, cheat me. Certainly I will take you, and at the university station I will be at the gate so nobody bothers you."

I went directly to the vice-chancellor and told him the whole story. And I told him, "I want to study philosophy, but it seems there is no freedom even to choose what I want to study. So you have to give me all the scholarships possible, because I will not be getting any financial help. Otherwise I *will* study philosophy, fasting ... even if I die."

He said, "No! Don't do that, because then the blame will be on me. I will give you all the scholarships."

From the very childhood we go on crippling, cutting freedoms; we try to make a child according to our desires. I was talking to a Christian missionary and he said, "God made man in his own image."

I said, "That is the foundation of all slavery. Why should God make man in his own image? Who is he? – and to give his own image to man means he has destroyed man from the very beginning." And that is what every father is doing.

Man's basic right is to be himself.

And in an authentic human society, everybody should be allowed to be himself – even if he chooses just to be a flute player, and he will not become the richest man in the world but will be a beggar on the streets.

Still I say freedom is so valuable.... You may not be the president of the country, you may be just a beggar playing the flute in the streets.

But you are yourself, and there is such deep contentment, fulfillment, that unless you know it you have missed the train.

Seventh: one earth, one humanity.

I don't see any reason at all why there should be so many nations. Why should there be so many lines on the map? And they are only on the map, remember. They are not on the earth; neither are they in the sky. And the map is man-made.

Existence has not created this earth in fragments.

I am reminded of one of my teachers. He was a very loving human being, and he had his own methods of teaching. He was a kind of rebel.

One day he came with a few pieces of cardboard, placed them on the table, and said to us all, "Look, this is the map of the world, but I have cut it into pieces and I have mixed them. Now anybody who is confident that he can put them in their right places and make the world map should come up."

One tried, failed; another tried, failed. I went on watching him and watching the people who were failing and why they were failing.

Watching five persons fail, I was the sixth. I went and I turned over all his cardboard pieces. He said, "What are you doing?"

I said, "You wait, I am working it out. Five people have failed but I have found the secret."

On the other side of the map was a picture of a man. I arranged the man, which was easier. On one side the man was arranged and on the other side the whole map of the world was arranged. That was the key that I had been looking for, waiting to see if I could get some clue. And when the others were arranging the pieces, I saw that there was something on the other side.

The teacher said, "You are a rascal! I was hoping you would come first, but when you didn't come I understood that you were waiting to find out the key. And you have found the right key."

The world is divided because man is divided; man is divided because the world is divided.

Start from anywhere; just let the whole of humanity be one, and the nations will disappear, the lines will disappear. It is our world – one humanity, one earth, and we can make it a paradise. Right now there is no need to describe hell. You can just look all around; it is here.

I have heard a story. A man died. He was a thief, a murderer, a rapist – you name it and he had done it. And when the angels started taking him away, he said, "Certainly you will be taking me to hell."

They said, "No."

He said, "What?"

They said, "You have been in hell; now we are taking you to heaven. The old hell is empty because you have created a *better* hell, so all the sinners are sent here." And the story seems to be significant. Looking around the earth, man is in such misery and suffering that there seems to be no need for another hell.

But we can change the whole situation. This earth can become a paradise. And then there will be no need for any paradise; paradise will be empty.

Eighth: uniqueness of every individual.

A very beautiful word has been misused so utterly that it is difficult to imagine, and that word is equality.

A few thinkers say human beings are equal. To counter them, the U.N. declares that equality is man's birthright. But nobody bothers to see that man is not equal and has never been equal. It is absolutely un-psychological.

Every man is unique.

The moment you are all equal you are a crowd, your individuality has been taken away. You are no longer yourself but just a cog in the wheel.

I teach not equality, not inequality – I teach uniqueness. Every individual is unique and needs to be respected in his uniqueness. Because every individiaul is unique, the birthright should be: equal opportunity for their growth of uniqueness.

It is such a simple and obvious fact. Two thousand years have passed and you have not been able to produce another Jesus.

Twenty-five centuries have passed and you have not been able to produce another Gautam Buddha; but you go on saying man is equal?

Man is unique, and everybody should be respected as a world in himself. He is neither inferior to anybody nor is he superior to anybody; he is alone.

In this aloneness there is beauty. You are no longer a mob, a crowd; you are yourself.

Ninth: a world government.

I am absolutely against governments. I am for one government for the whole world. That means no war will be possible; that means there will be no need to keep millions of people in armies unnecessarily. They can be productive, they can be helpful, and if they are merged into humanity, all poverty will disappear.

Right now seventy percent of the national income of every country goes to the army and the rest of the country lives on thirty percent. If armies disappear, seventy percent of the income of every country will be available. There is no need to be poor, there is no need to have any beggars.

These beggars, these Ethiopias – they are our creations. On the one hand, we are creating great armies and on the other hand, we are killing human beings through starvation. And these armies are doing nothing. They are simply professional killers, professional criminals, trained criminals. We are giving them training in how to kill.

And we talk about humanity, we talk about civilization, and still seventy percent of our income goes into killing.

One world government means a tremendous change, a revolution. The whole earth will be benefited by it.

Secondly, if there is one world government it becomes only functional. Right now government is not functional, it has real power. The president of a country or the prime minister of a country … in a functional government things will be different. Now you have the postmaster general; he is a functional person, he has no power. He has work, he has function, but he has no power. There is no need. The man who heads your railways, what power does he have? The man who is the president of your airlines, what power does he have? It is functional.

If there is only one government, it will automatically become functional. Right now it cannot be, because the fear of other governments keeps you afraid: "Make your leaders strong, give all support to the leaders." But if there is no war there is no need of anybody having power – war is the cause of power. And unless war disappears from the world, power cannot disappear; they are together.

A functional world government – like the post office, the railways, the airlines – will be efficient but without power. It will be a beautiful world where you don't know who the president is, who the prime minister is – they are your servants. Right now they have become your masters, and to keep their power they have to keep you always completely afraid. Pakistan is getting ready to fight with India, so you have to give all power to the Indian leaders. China is going to attack....

Adolf Hitler has written in his autobiography that if you want to remain in power, keep people always afraid. And he is absolutely right. Sometimes mad people are also right.

And tenth: meritocracy.

Democracy has failed.

We have lived under many kinds of governments – aristocracy, monarchy, city democracies – and now we have seen the whole world getting addicted to the idea of democracy. But democracy has not solved any problems; it has increased the problems.

It was because of these problems that a man like Karl Marx supported a dictatorship of the proletariat. I am not a supporter of a dictatorship of the proletariat, but I have another idea that goes far ahead of democracy.

Democracy means government by the people, of the people, for the people – but it is only in words. In India right now there are nine hundred million people. How can nine hundred million people have power? They have to delegate the power to somebody.

So it is not the people who rule, but the people who are chosen by them. What are your grounds for choosing? How do you manage to choose? And are you capable of choosing the right people? Have you been trained, educated for a democratic life? No, nothing has been done.

The ignorant masses can be exploited very easily by very insignificant things. For example, Nixon lost his election against Kennedy and the only reason was that Kennedy looked better on television than Nixon; this is the analysis of the psychoanalysts.

Nixon improved. When he discovered this, before the next election, he improved; he learned how to stand, how to walk, how to talk, how to dress. Even the color of your dress will make a difference on television. If you go there in white clothes you will look like a ghost.

Arbitrary reasons ... somebody speaks well, is a good orator. But that does not mean that he will make a good president. Somebody makes good shoes – do you think that will make him a good president?

It happened when Abraham Lincoln was chosen president. On the day of his inaugural address to the Senate, people were feeling very angry and hurt – because Lincoln's father was a shoemaker, and a shoemaker's son has defeated the great aristocrats. They were offended.

One arrogant aristocrat could not tolerate it. Before Lincoln started speaking, he said, "Wait a minute. Do you recognize me? You used to come with your father to my house sometimes because your father made shoes for my family. You used to help him." And the whole Senate laughed. This was an effort to humiliate Lincoln.

But you cannot humiliate people like Abraham Lincoln. He said, "I am very grateful to you that you reminded me of my dead father at this moment. Because my father was the best shoemaker in the whole country, and I know that I can never be the best president as he was the best shoemaker. He is still ahead of me."

What criterion do you use? How do you manage?

That's why my idea is that the days of democracy are over. A new kind of system is needed, based on merit. We have thousands of universities all over the world. Why have ordinary, unknowledgeable, ignorant masses choose people who will be holding tremendous power for five years in their hands? And now the power is so much that they can destroy the whole world.

Meritocracy means that only people who are educated in a certain area should be able to vote in that area. For example, only the educationists of the country should choose the education minister. Then you will have the best education minister possible. For the finance minister, you should choose somebody who knows finance, somebody who knows the complexities of economics. But this choice is possible only for people who are trained in economics, in financial matters – and there are thousands of people. For every post, the person who is chosen should be chosen by experts.

The health minister should be chosen by all the doctors, the surgeons, the medical experts, the scientists who are working in the medical field. Then we will have the cream of our genius, and we can depend on this cream to make the life of all humanity more peaceful, more blissful, more rich.

This idea I call a meritocracy. And once you have chosen all the people, then these people can choose the president and the prime minister. They will be our geniuses; they can choose the prime minister, the president, from the country, or they can choose from the members of the parliament. And for the parliament we should also make gradations.

For example, people who have at least a post-graduate degree should be able to vote. Just becoming twenty-one years old does not mean you are able to choose the right person. At twenty-one years, you don't know anything about life and its complexities. At least a post-graduate degree should be held by those who choose the members of the parliament or the senate or whatever you call it. In this way, we can make an educated, refined, cultured government.

Before the world government happens, each nation should pass through a meritocracy. And once we have enjoyed the fruits of a meritocracy then these people will be able to understand that if we can combine the whole world into one government, life can certainly be a joy, worth living – not to renounce, but to rejoice.

Up to now, whatever has happened has been accidental. Our history up to now is nothing but a history of accidents.

We have to stop this. Now we have to decide that the future is not going to be accidental. It will be created by us; and to create our world can be the greatest creation possible.

APPENDIX 1

UNIVERSAL DECLARATION OF HUMAN RIGHTS

Adopted and Proclaimed by
General Assembly Resolution 217 A (III)
of 10 December 1948 (*)

Preamble

Whereas recognition of the inherent dignity and of the equal and inalienable rights of all members of the human family is the foundation of freedom, justice and peace in the world,

Whereas disregard and contempt for human rights have resulted in barbarous acts which have outraged the conscience of mankind, and the advent of a world in which human beings shall enjoy freedom of speech and belief and freedom from fear and want has been proclaimed as the highest aspiration of the common people,

Whereas it is essential, if man is not to be compelled to have recourse, as a last resort, to rebellion against tyranny and oppression, that human rights should be protected by the rule of law,

Whereas it is essential to promote the development of friendly relations between nations,

Whereas the peoples of the United Nations have in the Charter reaffirmed their faith in fundamental human rights, in the dignity and worth of the human person and in the equal rights of men and women and have determined to promote social progress and better standards of life in larger freedom,

Whereas Member States have pledged themselves to achieve, in co-operation with the United Nations, the promotion of universal respect for and observance of human rights and fundamental freedoms,

Whereas a common understanding of these rights and freedoms is of the greatest importance for the full realization of this pledge,

(*) Voting: 48 for, including United States; 0 against; 8 abstentions (Eastern bloc, Saudi Arabia, and South Africa)

Now, therefore,

The General Assembly

Proclaims this Universal Declaration of Human Rights as a common standard of achievement for all peoples and all nations, to the end that every individual and every organ of society, keeping this Declaration constantly in mind, shall strive by teaching and education to promote respect for these rights and freedoms and by progressive measures, national and international, to secure their universal and effective recognition and observance, both among the peoples of Member States themselves and among the peoples of territories under their jurisdiction.

Article 1

All human beings are born free and equal in dignity and rights. They are endowed with reason and conscience and should act towards one another in a spirit of brotherhood.

Article 2

Everyone is entitled to all the rights and freedoms set forth in this Declaration, without distinction of any kind, such as race, color, sex, language, religion, political or other opinion, national or social origin, property, birth or other status.

Furthermore, no distinction shall be made on the basis of the political, jurisdictional or international status of the country or territory to which a person belongs, whether it be independent, trust, non-self-governing or under any other limitation of sovereignty.

Article 3

Everyone has the right to life, liberty and security of person.

Article 4

No one shall be held in slavery or servitude; slavery and the slave trade shall be prohibited in all their forms.

Article 5

No one shall be subjected to torture or to cruel, inhuman or degrading treatment or punishment.

Article 6

Everyone has the right to recognition everywhere as a person before the law.

Article 7

All are equal before the law and are entitled without any discrimination to equal protection of the law. All are entitled to equal protection against any discrimination in violation of this Declaration and against any incitement to such discrimination.

Article 8

Everyone has the right to an effective remedy by the competent national tribunals for acts violating the fundamental rights granted him by the constitution or by law.

Article 9

No one shall be subjected to arbitrary arrest, detention or exile.

Article 10

Everyone is entitled in full equality to a fair and public hearing by an independent and impartial tribunal, in the determination of his rights and obligations and of any criminal charge against him.

Article 11

1. Everyone charged with a penal offence has the right to be presumed innocent until proved guilty according to law in a public trial at which he has had all the guarantees necessary for his defence.
2. No one shall be held guilty of any penal offence on account of any act or omission which did not constitute a penal offence, under

national or international law, at the time when it was committed. Nor shall a heavier penalty be imposed than the one that was applicable at the time the penal offense was committed.

Article 12

No one shall be subjected to arbitrary interference with his privacy, family, home or correspondence, nor to attacks upon his honor and reputation. Everyone has the right to the protection of the law against such interference or attacks.

Article 13

1. Everyone has the right to freedom of movement and residence within the borders of each State.
2. Everyone has the right to leave any country, including his own, and to return to his country.

Article 14

1. Everyone has the right to seek and to enjoy in other countries asylum from persecution.
2. This right may not be invoked in the case of prosecutions genuinely arising from non-political crimes or from acts contrary to the purposes and principles of the United Nations.

Article 15

1. Everyone has the right to a nationality.
2. No one shall be arbitrarily deprived of his nationality nor denied the right to change his nationality.

Article 16

1. Men and women of full age, without any limitation due to race, nationality or religion, have the right to marry and to found a family. They are entitled to equal rights as to marriage, during marriage and its dissolution.
2. Marriage shall be entered into only with the free and full consent of the intending spouses.

3. The family is the natural and fundamental group unit of society and is entitled to protection by society and the State.

Article 17

1. Everyone has the right to own property alone as well as in association with others.
2. No one shall be arbitrarily deprived of his property.

Article 18

Everyone has the right to freedom of thought, conscience and religion; this right includes freedom to change his religion or belief, and freedom, either alone or in community with others and in public or private to manifest his religion or belief in teaching, practice, worship and observance.

Article 19

Everyone has the right to freedom of opinion and expression; this right includes freedom to hold opinions without interference and to seek, receive and impart information and ideas through any media and regardless of frontiers.

Article 20

1. Everyone has the right to freedom of peaceful assembly and association.
2. No one may be compelled to belong to an association.

Article 21

1. Everyone has the right to take part in the government of his country, directly or through freely chosen representatives.
2. Everyone has the right of equal access to public services in his country.
3. The will of the people shall be the basis of the authority of government; this will shall be expressed in periodic and genuine elections which shall be by universal and equal suffrage and shall be held by secret vote or by equivalent free voting procedures.

Article 22

Everyone, as a member of society, has the right to social security and is entitled to realization, through national effort and international cooperation and in accordance with the organization and resources of each State, of the economic, social and cultural rights indispensable for his dignity and the free development of his personality.

Article 23

1. Everyone has the right to work, to free choice of employment, to just and favorable conditions of work and to protection against unemployment.
2. Everyone, without any discrimination, has the right to equal pay for equal work.
3. Everyone who works has the right to just and favorable remuneration ensuring for himself and his family an existence worthy of human dignity, and supplemented, if necessary, by other means of social protection.
4. Everyone has the right to form and to join trade unions for the protection of his interests.

Article 24

Everyone has the right to rest and leisure, including reasonable limitation of working hours and periodic holidays with pay.

Article 25

1. Everyone has the right to a standard of living adequate for the health and well-being of himself and of his family, including food, clothing, housing and medical care and of necessary social services, and the right to security in the event of unemployment, sickness, disability, widowhood, old age or other lack of likelihood in circumstances beyond his control.
2. Motherhood and childhood are entitled to special care and assistance. All children, whether born in or out of wedlock, shall enjoy the same social protection.

Article 26

1. Everyone has the right to education. Education shall be free, at least in the elementary and fundamental stages. Elementary education shall be made compulsory. Technical and professional education shall be made generally available and higher education shall be equally accessible to all on the basis of merit.

2. Education shall be directed to the full development of the human personality and to the strengthening of respect for human rights and fundamental freedoms. It shall promote understanding, tolerance and friendship among all nations, racial or religious groups, and shall further the activities of the United Nations for the maintenance of peace.

3. Parents have a prior right to choose the kind of education that shall be given to their children.

Article 27

1. Everyone has the right freely to participate in the cultural life of the community, to enjoy the arts and to share in scientific advancement and its benefits.

2. Everyone has the right to the protection of the moral and material interests resulting from any scientific, literary or artistic production of which he is the author.

Article 28

Everyone is entitled to a social and international order in which the rights and freedoms set forth in this Declaration can be fully realized.

Article 29

1. Everyone has duties to the community in which alone the free and full development of his personality is possible.

2. In the exercise of his rights and freedoms, everyone shall be subject only to such limitations as are determined by law solely for the purpose of securing due recognition and respect for the rights and freedoms of others and of meeting the just requirement of morality, public order and the general welfare in a democratic society.

APPENDIX 2

SOME BIOGRAPHICAL FACTS AND EVENTS FROM THE LIFE OF BHAGWAN SHREE RAJNEESH

The Childhood Years

1931 Bhagwan Shree Rajneesh was born in Kuchwada, Madhya Pradesh, India, on December 11, 1931, the eldest son of a modest cloth merchant who belonged to the Jain religion. He spent His first seven years with His grandparents who allowed Him absolute freedom to do exactly as He liked, and who fully supported His early and intense investigations into the truth about life.

1938 After the death of His grandfather, He went to live with His parents at Gadawara, a town of 20,000. His grandmother moved to the same town and remained His most generous friend until she died in 1970, declaring herself to be a disciple of her grandson.

1946 Bhagwan experienced His first satori at 14 years of age. Over the years, His experiments with meditation deepened. The intensity of His spiritual search took its toll on His physical condition. His parents and friends feared He might not live long.

The University Years

1952 At the age of 21, on March 21, 1953, Bhagwan attained enlightenment, the highest peak of human consciousness. Here, He said, His outer biography ended, and He has since lived in an egoless state of at-oneness with the inner laws of life. Outwardly, He continued to pursue His studies at the University of Jabalpur, from which He graduated with First Class Honours in Philosophy in 1956. He was All-India Debating Champion and won the Gold Medal in His graduating class.

1957 Bhagwan taught at the Sanskrit College, Raipur. A year later, He became philosophy professor at the University of Jabalpur. He gave up this post in 1966 in order to dedicate Himself entirely to the task of teaching modern man the art of meditation. Throughout the sixties, He traveled the length and breadth of India as the "Acharya (teacher) Rajneesh," arousing the wrath of the Establishment wherever He went. He exposed the hypocrisy of the vested interests and their attempts to obstruct man's access to his greatest human right – the right to be himself. He addressed audiences of tens of thousands of people, touching the hearts of millions.

The Bombay Years

1968 He settled in Bombay, living and teaching there. Regularly, He held "meditation camps," mostly in hill stations, where He introduced His revolutionary Dynamic Meditation, a technique that helps to stop the mind by first allowing it to cathart. From 1970 He started initiating people into Neo-Sannyas, a path of commitment to self-exploration and meditation, helped by His love and personal guidance. He began to be called "Bhagwan" - "The Blessed One."

1970 The first seekers from the West arrived, among them many professional people. Bhagwan's fame began to spread throughout Europe, America, Australia and Japan. The monthly Meditation Camps continued and in 1974 a new place was found in Poona, where the teaching could be intensified.

The Poona Years

1974 On the 21st anniversary of Bhagwan's enlightenment, the ashram in Poona opened. The radius of Bhagwan's influence became worldwide. At the same time, His health began to fail seriously. Bhagwan retreated more and more into the privacy of His room, emerging only twice daily: lecturing in the morning and initiating and advising seekers in the evenings.

Therapy groups combining Eastern insight into meditation with Western psychotherapy were created. Withing two years, the ashram earned a reputation as "the world's finest growth and therapy center." Bhagwan's lectures encompassed all the great religious traditions of the world. At the same time, His vast erudition in Western science and thought, His clarity of speech and depth of argument make the time-honored gap between East and West disappear for His listeners. His lectures, taped and transcribed into books, fill hundreds of volumes and have been absorbed by hundreds of thousands of readers. By the late seventies, Bhagwan's ashram in Poona had become a mecca to modern seekers of truth.

Indian Prime Minister Morarji Desai, a devout traditional Hindu, thwarted all attempts of Bhagwan's disciples to move their ashram to a remote corner of India where they would be able to experiment with applying Bhagwan's teachings to create a self-sufficient community living in meditation, love, creativity and laughter.

1980 An attempt was made to murder Bhagwan at one of His lectures by a member of a traditional Hindu sect. While the official religions and churches opposed Him East and West, Bhagwan by then had over a quarter of a million disciples worldwide.

A New Phase - Rajneeshpuram, USA

1981 On May 1st Bhagwan stopped speaking and entered a phase of "silent heart-to-heart communion" while His body, now seriously ill from a back condition, was resting. He was taken to the USA by His doctors and caretakers in view of possible emergency surgery. His American disciples purchased a 64,000 acre ranch in the Central Oregon desert. They invited Bhawgan there - where He recovered rapidly. A model agricultural commune evolved around Him with breathtaking speed and impressive results, reclaiming overgrazed and depleted land from the desert and turning it into a green oasis feeding a city of 5,000.

At yearly summer festivals held for Bhagwan's friends all over the world, up to 20,000 visitors were housed and fed at this new city of Rajneeshpuram.

Parallel to the rapid growth of the commune in Oregon, large communes sprang up in all major Western countries, including Japan, living on their own independent businesses. Bhagwan had by then applied for permanent residence in the U.S. as a religious leader, but was refused by the American government; one of the reasons given was His vow of public silence. At the same time the new city was under increasing legal attack from the Oregon government and the Christian majority in the state. Oregon's land use laws, meant to protect the environment, became a major weapon in the fight against a city that had put enormous effort into reclaiming barren land and enhancing the environment – in fact a city which had become an ecological model for the world.

In October 1984, Bhagwan started speaking to small groups in His residence, and in July 1985 He started giving public discourses every morning to thousands of seekers in Rajneesh Mandir.

1985 On September 14, Bhagwan's personal secretary and several members of the commune's management suddenly left, and a whole pattern of illegal acts committed by them came to light. Bhagwan invited the American authorities to the city to fully investigate the matter. The authorities used this opportunity to accelerate their fight against the commune.

On October 29, Bhagwan was arrested without a warrant in Charlotte, NC. At the bail hearings He was put in chains. The trip back to Oregon where He was to appear in court – normally a five hour flight – took eight days. For a few days there was no trace of Bhagwan. Later He revealed that in the Oklahoma State Penitentiary He was signed in under the name of "David Washington" and put into an isolation cell with a prisoner suffering from infectious herpes, a disease that could have proven fatal for Bhagwan.

Just an hour before being finally released, after a 12-day ordeal in prisons and chains, a bomb was discovered at the Portland, Oregon maximum security jail in which Bhagwan was kept. Everybody was evacuated except Bhagwan, who was kept inside for an hour.

In mid-November His lawyers urged Him to plead guilty to two of thirty-four minor "immigration violations" with which He had been charged, so as to avoid further risks to His life in the hands of the American judicial system. Bhagwan acquiesced and entered an "Alfred plea," a plea peculiar to the US judicial system, whereby He could accept the contention of guilt while at the same maintain His innocence. He was fined four hundred thousand dollars and ordered to leave the USA, not to return for five years. He left by private jet the same day and flew to India, where He rested in the Himalayas.

A week later, the Oregon commune decided to disperse.

In a press conference, U.S. Attorney Charles Turner made three telling points in answering the question: Why weren't the charges brought against His secretary also brought against Bhagwan?

Turner said that the government's first priority was to destroy the commune and that the authorities knew that the removal of Bhagwan would precipitate this. Second, they did not want to make Bhagwan a martyr. Third, there was no evidence whatsoever implicating Him in any of the crimes.

A STUDY TOUR IN HUMAN RIGHTS

Dec.85 Bhagwan's new secretary, His companion and His doctor were ordered out of India, their visas cancelled. Bhagwan left for Kathmandu, Nepal, where He resumed His daily discourses.

Feb.86 Bhagwan goes to *Greece* on a 30-day tourist visa, where He lived in the villa of a Greek film producer and started to speak twice daily. Disciples flocked to hear Him. The Greek Orthodox clergy threatened the Greek government that blood will flow unless Bhagwan is thrown out of the country.

Mar.5 '86 Police broke into the villa and arrested Bhagwan without warrant, shunting Him off to Athens where only a twenty-five thousand dollar sum can move the authorities not to put Him on the boat to India

Mar.6 '86 He left in a private jet for *Switzerland* where His 7-day visa was cancelled by armed policemen upon arrival. He was declared 'persona non grata' because of "immigration offenses in the United States" and asked to leave.

He moved on to *Sweden* where He was met the same way – surrounded by rifled policemen. He was told He was "a danger to national security," and ordered to leave immediately.

He moved on to *England*. His pilots were now legally bound to rest for eight hours. Bhagwan wanted to wait in the First Class Transit Lounge, but He was not allowed; nor was He allowed to stay in a hotel overnight. Instead, He and His companions were locked up in a small, dirty cell crowded with refugees.

Mar.7 '86 Bhagwan and His group flew to *Ireland*, where they were given tourist visas. They went to a hotel near Limerick. The next morning police arrived and ordered them to leave immediately. However, this was not possible because *Canada* had by then refused Bhagwan's plane permission to land at Gander for refueling on the intended flight to *Antigua* in the Carribean.

This extraordinary denial of the right to refuel was made in spite of a bond from Lloyds of London guaranteeing that Bhagwan would not step outside the plane.

On the condition that there was no publicity that might embarrass the authorities, He was allowed to remain in Ireland until other arrangements could be made.

During the wait, Antigua withdrew permission for Bhagwan to go there. *Holland,* when asked, also refused Bhagwan. *Germany* had already passed a 'preventive decree' not to allow Bhagwan to enter their country. In *Italy,* His tourist application remained stalled – and is still stalled 10 months later....

Mar.19 '86 At the last moment, *Uruguay* turned up with an invitation, and so, on March 19th, Bhagwan, His lovers and fellow travelers flew to Montevideo via Dakar, Senegal.

Uruguay even opened up the possibility of permanent residence. However, in Uruguay it was discovered why He was being denied access to every country He tried to enter – telexes with "diplomatic secret information" (all from NATO government sources) mentioning INTERPOL rumors of "smuggling charges, drug dealing and prostitution" concerning Bhagwan's circle had invariably preceded them in their prospective host countries just in time for the police to be alerted. Uruguay soon came under the same pressure.

May 14 '86 The government planned to announce at a press conference that Bhagwan had been granted permanent residence in Uruguay.

That night Sanguinetti, the President of Uruguay, received a call from Washington, DC, saying that if Bhagwan stayed in Uruguay, current US loans of six billion dollars would be called in, and no future loans given. Bhagwan had to leave Uruguay on June 18th.

The next day, Sanguinetti and Reagan announced from Washington a new US loan to Uruguay of one hundred and fifty million dollars.

Jun.19 '86 *Jamaica* granted Bhagwan a 10-day visa. Moments after He landed there, a US navy jet landed next to Bhagwan's private jet, and two civilians descended. The next morning, the visas of Bhagwan and His group were cancelled.

Bhagwan flew on to Lisbon via Madrid, and remained "undiscovered" for some time. A few weeks later policemen were placed around the villa where He was resting. Bhagwan decided to return back to India the next day.

In all, twenty-one countries had either deported Him or denied Him entry.

Jul.29 '86 Bhagwan arrived in Bombay, India, where He settled for six months as a personal guest of an Indian friend. In the privacy of His host's home, He resumed His daily discourses.

Jan.4 '87 — Bhagwan moved into the house at the ashram in Poona where He had lived for the major part of the seventies.

Immediately upon Bhagwan's arrival, the police chief of Poona ordered Him to leave on the grounds that He was a "controversial person" who may "disturb the tranquility of the city." The order was revoked the same day by the Bombay High Court. The same Hindu fanatic who, in May 1980, tried to murder Bhagwan by throwing a knife at Him during a public lecture began making aggressive threats about forcing his way into the ashram with 200 commandoes trained in martial arts – unless Bhagwan was expelled from Poona.

Feb.1 '87 — At the time of writing, the Indian authorities are becoming increasingly belligerent, refusing visas to His foreign lovers and fellow travelers, and placing Bhagwan under virtual house arrest.

The governments of the "free world" have thus conspired to isolate Bhagwan in "internal exile."

For further information contact:
RAJNEESH FOUNDATION EUROPE
Rennweg 34
CH 8001 Zürich
SWITZERLAND